Everything You Need to Know About

WEAPONS
IN SCHOOL
AND AT HOME

After a shooting at Jefferson High School in New York City, police set up a barricade and reinforced security.

• THE NEED TO KNOW LIBRARY •

Everything You Need to Know About

WEAPONS
IN SCHOOL
AND AT HOME

Jay Schleifer

THE ROSEN PUBLISHING GROUP, INC.
NEW YORK

Published in 1994 by The Rosen Publishing Group, Inc.
29 East 21st Street, New York, NY 10010

First Edition
Copyright 1994 by The Rosen Publishing Group, Inc.

Manufactured in the United States of America.

Library of Congress Cataloging-in-Publication Data

Schleifer, Jay
    Everything you need to know about weapons in school and at home / Jay
Schleifer. — 1st ed.
        p.   cm. — (The Need to know library)
    Includes bibliographical references and index.
    ISBN 0-8239-1531-X
    1. Gun control—United States 2. Firearms ownership—United States. 3.
School violence—United States. 4. Firearms—Safety measures. 5. Weapons—
Safety measures. I. Title. II. Title: Weapons in school and at home. III. Series.
HV436.S35 1994
363.3'3'0973—dc20   93-41940
                                            CIP
                                             AC

Contents

Introduction:

Note from the Author

Dear Reader:

It may seem unusual to begin a book like this with a personal story from the author's family, but I think you'll see why we have chosen to do so. The story in Chapter 1 is about a young woman named Laura. Laura is my daughter. Not long ago, she was about your age, going to a junior high school probably a lot like yours.

Hopefully, what happened to her at that school will never happen to you.

Here's the story, told by Laura herself. Most of the names and dates have been changed. The rest of the story is frighteningly true.

Jay Schleifer

Chapter 1

Death in Sixth Period: A True Story

January 12, 1988, was cloudy and a little chilly, but nothing unusual for winter in New England. It was just a regular day in the 7th grade at our junior high school—or so I thought.

Then something bizarre happened—right in the middle of sixth-period English class—that turned this ordinary day into the most frightening experience of my life.

I remember it clearly, even though it happened years ago. Our teacher had just handed back the quizzes we'd taken the day before, when suddenly the classroom door flew open.

There stood Charlie C., well known as the "bad boy" of the eighth grade. Only today he wasn't lugging his usual giant boombox radio around . Instead, he had what looked like a plastic toy gun slung over his right shoulder.

What was going on? Why was Charlie fooling around? Charlie's gun couldn't be real—could it? Things like that didn't happen in our small, quiet town. Weapons were only found in big city schools, right?

Wrong. We soon learned that the gun was real. That morning, Charlie had been suspended by the principal, Mr. Davis, for refusing to take his hat off in the building! Charlie vowed he'd come back and kill the principal.

Mr. Davis had been a school official for many years. In that time, he'd heard threats from a lot of angry kids. But this one was for real. When Charlie got home, he broke into his grandfather's gun collection, took out one of the guns, loaded it, and started back to school.

When Charlie returned, he headed straight for the main office. His first shot went through a hallway window, missing Mr. Davis, but hitting a secretary in the arm. Mr. Davis was cut by flying glass.

Bill, the school janitor, happened to be in that part of the building at the time of the shooting. The young father of two was well liked in our school. The kids considered him a friend. Bill asked Charlie what he was doing. When Charlie refused to answer, Bill said, "I'll have to call the police."

Cornered, frightened, and half-crazy, Charlie pulled the trigger—several times. Bill died at Charlie's feet, in a pool of blood on the floor he'd polished only hours before.

Many innocent bystanders have been victims of gunfire in the streets and schools.

Now Charlie, a murderer at age 13, stood at our classroom door. He was looking for a way out. He tried grabbing the teacher as a hostage. Just then a boy near the door jumped from his seat, yelling "Take me! Take me!"

At first, the boy thought it was all a big joke. He went on laughing as Charlie paraded him in the hallway. But soon we heard sirens, and a loud voice over the P.A. system ordering Charlie to drop the gun. The boy began to cry. It was no joke.

The teacher screamed for all of us to crouch behind her big wooden desk in the corner of the room. As we huddled there, I looked at my classmates. Some were sobbing, some were too stunned to cry.

During the next two hours, Charlie roamed the hall and classrooms like an animal on the loose. One moment he was yelling threats, and the next moment, crying. He was clearly "losing it."

The police tried everything to persuade Charlie to give himself up. They finally found Charlie's aunt and rushed her to school. She pleaded with Charlie over the P.A. system.

"I can't!" Charlie screamed back. "Don't you see that I can't!"

After what seemed like forever, Charlie caved in. He shoved the boy clear. Then he walked to the window and tossed the gun out.

Officers charged in immediately, jumped Charlie, and pinned him to the floor. One officer shoved a gun to the side of his head as others handcuffed him. It was over. Meanwhile, the vice principal, not knowing if there were other shooters, started screaming, "Get out! Get out of the building!"

We ran down the empty halls and headed outside—right into 200 cops pointing loaded guns at us. Practically every news reporter in the state was there. Our quiet little world had been turned upside down!

That night, all three major TV networks reported the story about our school. By morning, we were on almost every front page in the nation. It was the most fame the school, or the town, had ever had. But it wasn't the kind of fame anyone wanted. School was closed the next day for Bill's funeral. The day after that was spent talking in class about all that had happened.

In time, things settled down. Charlie was locked up in the toughest part of the state juvenile center. They'll hold him there as long as the law allows.

The principal retired not long after the incident. My teacher, who was sort of a hero, still gives English quizzes in the same room. And the kid who was taken hostage went on to graduate with honors.

For me, nothing was ever quite the same. It's one thing to read about guns in someone else's school. It's another to have your own young life in the hands of an out-of-control teenager. But at least I did live through it.

Bill the Janitor did not.

Laura Schleifer

A variety of handguns and other weapons can be bought in stores.

Chapter 2

A World of Weapons

The gun that killed the janitor and wounded another person is part of a growing problem in homes and schools alike. The problem is weapons in the hands of young people.

Most any item can be used as a *weapon*, even if it was not made for that purpose. Bricks, bottles, baseball bats, and, at times, hands and feet are used to hurt people. But it's the items that are *designed* to hurt people—like switchblade knives, "Oriental fighting sticks," and of course, guns—that cause the most damage.

In the U.S., guns are the second greatest killer of high-school-aged youngsters. (Car crashes are the number-one killer.) Guns are also the *fastest-growing* cause of death in this age group. For every 10 young Americans who died from gunfire in the 1970s, about 17 die in the 1990s.

Six Deaths a Day, Every Day!

According to the U.S. government, between 2,000 and 3,000 young people die from gunshot wounds each year. That's an average of more than six a day. And depending on what ages are included, some sources say the death rate could be twice that.

Half of those young people are murdered. The rest die in gun-related accidents or because they use guns to kill themselves. Thousands more are wounded by gunfire. It is also disturbing to discover that teens themselves (ages 14–17) now commit murder at a faster rate than adults!

Guns are only part of the problem. Other kinds of weapons are harder to keep track of. But for every gun attack, there are said to be about five knife attacks.

You may be asking yourself why society hasn't banded together to rid itself of all weapons and the threat they represent. To understand, you need to look more closely at the special place weapons— and especially guns—have in American society.

"Make My Day!"

We live in a world of weapons. You don't need to look very far to see how widespread and accepted they are.

Start by turning your TV on. Incidents involving weapons are sure to be on the news. Many times these stories are discussed even before important world events. Program directors say that reports about violence seem to be the most interesting ones to many TV viewers.

Or perhaps you tune in to any number of action shows or movies about crime and the police. An example of such movies comes from superstar Clint Eastwood's successful "Dirty Harry" series. In it, Eastwood, playing a tough police hero, stares down the sight of a powerful gun he's pointing at the bad guy and says the now-famous words, "Go ahead, make my day!"

The next time you walk through one of the large toy stores, head for the "Action Toys" department. You'll probably find an assortment of toy guns and rifles, bows and arrows, plastic swords, knives, grenades, and space weapons.

There's really nothing new about all this. In America, weapons have always been an important part of life and somewhat glorified in children's play. Native Americans used the bow and arrow, spear, and lance to hunt and to protect themselves against unfriendly neighbors. They celebrated their weapons in traditional dances and decorated them as pieces of art.

The first European settlers brought guns with them to America. Later, settlers used their guns to fight the British in the Revolutionary War. Then people moved westward. Anyone who's ever seen a cowboy movie knows something about the "Wild West." It is shown as a place where most males had a "six-shooter" hanging from their belt or a rifle in their saddlebag. That's probably stretching the truth a bit. But even the famous gunmaker, Colt Firearms, calls its .45 caliber revolver "The Gun That Won the West."

Weapons in Other Nations

Other nations have a tradition of weapons, too. But it's more a matter of honoring their military forces than arming their private citizens. The British, for example, don't normally arm their police officers. Instead, British "coppers" patrol their beat with only a nightstick for protection. Amazing as it may seem, British criminals seem to play by the same rules. For the most part, they do not use guns in their crimes.

The nations of the Far East invented both the martial arts, such as karate and kung fu, and unusual weapons, such as fighting stars and sticks. Many martial arts movies show the training and the discipline necessary to master these ways of fighting, but they fail to explain the rules and philosophy behind many of the martial arts. They do not make it clear that for many, violence is used only for self-defense. It is considered the last step to be taken when there is no other way to solve matters peacefully.

But things may be changing in other nations, as well. Weapons violence seems to be on the rise. Some people blame U.S. TV shows and movies. As this kind of entertainment spreads worldwide and

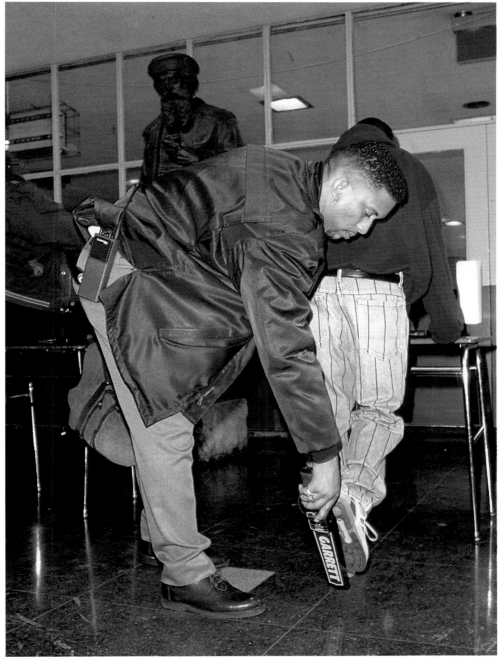

Security measures in schools include searches for weapons with metal detectors.

becomes more popular, critics fear that weapons violence may increase along with it.

Is Seeing Believing?

It's been calculated that American kids see about 200,000 acts of violence and 25,000 murders on TV by the time they reach age 18. Some experts fear that seeing this much violence teaches young people that hurting or killing is an easy way to solve problems, or that weapons and killing are somehow not real. (One teenage gang member wounded in a shootout was amazed at how much the gunshot hurt. After all, on TV, people who get shot never show much pain!)

Others say that most young people can easily tell the difference between what's real and what's make-believe. They remind us that millions of TV watchers grow up normally without being troubled or influenced by the violence they see. But nobody really knows the long-term effects of viewing so much violence. It's scary to think that acts of violence on TV may cause the very same acts to happen in real life.

This, however, *is* fact: The "tools of violence" are all around today's youngsters. There are about 60 million private owners of guns in the United States alone. They own some 200 million firearms.

That means there are almost as many guns in America as there are people— a gun in about half the homes in America!

Some students feel they need guns for self-protection.

Taking a Chance

Many people agree that guns in themselves are not bad. Most guns in private hands are meant for hunting or sports shooting, not hurting people. Some are in private collections. And other weapons are kept by their owners for protection against crime. The vast majority of weapons never cause a problem.

But where there's a weapon, there's always the *chance* that it may get into the wrong hands and be used for the wrong purpose. That means there's always a need for the owner of that weapon to take extra precautions to make sure this doesn't happen.

Many people believe that every citizen has a right to have a gun either for hunting or self-defense.

Chapter 3

The Right to Bear Arms

Because weapons are so much a part of life, they can be legally owned in most nations. In fact, the U.S. even has a major law that *protects* a private citizen's right to own a gun.

The law, which dates back to 1791, is found in the Second Amendment of the U.S. Constitution, and is often known as "The Right to Bear Arms." It's part of the Bill of Rights, the same list of laws that grants Americans freedom of speech and religion. The law says that citizens should always have the right to keep guns so they'll always be able to defend their freedom.

It's pretty clear *why* the law was passed when it was. The Americans had just used weapons to gain their independence from England. They had fought the British in the Revolutionary War and wanted to secure their future.

But that's not all the law says. It *also* says these guns should be kept because the nation needs to have a "militia." A militia means a part-time army of citizens, like the National Guard, called upon for service in times of emergency. Such organizations keep their guns locked up in a central place.

Some Americans believe that lawmakers in the 1700s did not mean for private citizens to own guns when they weren't serving in the militia.

Others believe that the lawmakers did intend for private citizens to keep arms, and to take their guns with them to serve in the militia. What did the Founding Fathers mean? They can't tell us. They've been dead for over 100 years!

The Great Gun-Control Debate

The issue is gun control, and the following arguments present the pros and cons of the debate.

Pro

Those who are *for* gun control favor the banning of privately owned guns. They believe the result will be a huge drop in violence and the saving of many lives. Not only would accidents be prevented if there were no legally owned guns, but it would be harder for criminals to get hold of guns. If there are fewer guns in public hands, there are fewer guns to steal. All of society would benefit. Gun-control advocates believe that the enormous cost of police, medical, and social services needed to deal with gun-related problems would drop sharply.

Con

Those who are *against* gun control favor private ownership of guns. They often point out that "guns don't kill, people do." They see violent people as the real problem. And they claim that if there were no guns in the hands of the public, such dangerous people would find other weapons.

What's more, gun-owner groups feel that banning guns would have no effect on criminal use. Criminals own guns now! They won't change their ways just because the laws change. These groups point out that if legally owned guns were banned, only the criminals would have weapons. Lawful citizens would be unprotected.

The gun-owner groups think that the answer to the problem of accidents with weapons lies in better training and safety. They ask why gun owners who practice weapons safety should be made to suffer because other gun owners are careless.

The Law Stands

This debate has gone on for years. There are powerful organizations on each side, spending millions of dollars to convince lawmakers and the public that their view is the right one.

But whenever gun-control laws have been put forward, the courts have allowed The Right to Bear Arms to stand. Private gun ownership is legal— under certain conditions—one of which directly affects young people.

Limits to the Law

Here are some of the conditions for private ownership of guns:

• No one can privately own automatic weapons, like *assault-style* weapons, that fire a steady stream of bullets when the trigger is pulled, without a hard-to-get special permit. Other heavy army-type weapons also require special permits.

• A person with a serious criminal record or record of mental illness can't legally own a firearm. By law, a person seeking to buy weapons almost always has to undergo a background check. In some places, this involves waiting for several days. In others, it's done right in the gun store.

• Certain cheaply made handguns and especially damaging bullets, often called "cop-killer" bullets, are outlawed.

• Some local areas have other special laws, often about carrying *concealed* weapons. These are weapons that are hidden from view. Schools and businesses have the right to make their own rules about banning weapons.

• No one under 18 can legally own a gun of any kind.

People mourn the death of a young teen who was shot and killed in school.

In other nations, such as Canada, Great Britain, and Japan, there is no built-in right to own guns. A private owner needs a permit to own one. To get a gun permit a person needs a valid reason, such as a job as a bank guard.

Can All Weapons Be Banned?

When it comes to other weapons, such as knives, the law is less clear. Certain kinds of knives, such as "switchblades," have been made illegal. But the problem with regular knives is that there's no way to control the use of everyday tools. Knives can be used for cutting food as easily as they can be used to hurt people. The same is true of axes, clubs, bats, hammers, and other common household or workplace objects.

The law usually works by *making the penalty greater* if someone uses a weapon in a crime, than if no weapon is used. Armed robbery can result in more jail time than simple robbery. Assault (attack on a person) with a deadly weapon is a far more serious crime than simple assault. And that's even if the weapon used turns out to be a common kitchen knife, ice pick, or bicycle chain.

It seems likely that there will always be weapons around young people. More laws cannot guarantee public safety. What can the owners of those weapons, other adults, and young people do to keep kids from dying or being hurt? Ask yourself what *you* can do in your own neighborhood.

Chapter 4

Weapons in the Home

*M*ary, a single mom, had bought a small pistol
for what she thought were good reasons. There'd been
break-ins in the area and teen gangs were moving in.
Every night the TV news reported more frightening
stories of growing violence in the neighborhood. Mary
promised herself that violence would not touch her
family—not as long as she could protect them!

During the day, she kept the gun in her purse. At
night, she loaded it and put it in the bedside drawer.
Mary was prepared.

At 2 o'clock one morning, it seemed all her night-
mares were coming true. There were sounds in the
kitchen. When Mary heard a crash she grabbed the
gun. She ran in the darkness and fired at the noise.
She turned on the lights, and screamed. Mary had
shot her own eight-year-old daughter! The child had
gotten out of bed looking for a glass of water.

Pete was furious. Final grades were out, and his were not good. The coach benched him just before the big game. Pete's dad got mad and grounded him for the rest of the semester. Now Pete wouldn't even see the big game. Gloria, his girlfriend, would be there— maybe with somebody else.

Pete decided he'd make them all suffer. His dad's gun cabinet was never locked, so he pulled a weapon out and loaded it. For a long time, Pete sat and looked at the sleek, black-barreled gun. Then he sat down and wrote a short note. Finally, he put the gun to his head, and pulled the trigger.

Terri and Paul had been married just a year, but the honeymoon was clearly over. They fought all the time, usually over money or their families. Most of their friends felt that the marriage would end, but not the way it did—with Terri stabbing Paul with one of his own hunting knives.

Ed came home from school and found the usual note from his mom about doing chores and home- work. But on this day, he had something else to do first. He asked his friend Jeff over so he could show him his dad's new gun. Ed got the gun out of the closet where he had seen his father put it. He unpacked the weapon and pointed it at Jeff, making the same noises he made when he played with his toy gun. But there was a real gun noise and Jeff fell to the floor. Later, Ed told the police, "It just went off in my hands!"

Owning and carrying a gun may give one a false sense of security.

If owning weapons is supposed to help people feel safe in their homes, it doesn't always work out that way.

In fact, studies show it's 12 times more likely that a young person will be *hurt* by a weapon at home than protected by it. It's also more likely that the weapon will be in the hands of someone the youngster knows (or his or her own hands) than in any stranger's.

Accidents

The army term "smart weapons" doesn't always apply to the weapons people have in their homes. Nor does the word "smart" apply to some of their owners! If there's a careless way to store or handle weapons, someone is already doing it.

Guns are often left out in the open. Even with small children around, many gun owners leave their weapons in convenient spots. Sometimes the owner shows a child exactly where he or she is putting a gun, then says "Don't ever open this drawer and touch this." These words, of course, make the youngster curious. As soon as the adult is away, the youngster heads for the forbidden drawer.

Weapons are left loaded. Some people want to be prepared for the unexpected. Parents may think they are being careful by removing the bullet-storage unit (cartridge clip). But many people forget to remove the ready-to-fire round already in the gun's firing chamber. Thinking the weapon is unloaded, people who pick it up are not always careful handling it.

Acting out of fear. An untrained person who buys a gun for protection may react to sights and sounds too quickly. He or she may think there is a prowler and fire at the wrong target. This happens more often than most people think. In one study of guns used for protection, only about 15 percent of the shots were directed at the intended targets.

What do you call harmless? Many people consider air rifles, sometimes called "BB guns," harmless. They think of them as toys. Adults buy them for children or teens, to use in target shooting or for hunting small animals. And often there are no laws to control who buys them or what age group they are bought for.

At one time, air rifles were fairly low-powered. If someone was shot by one, that person would feel a sting and get a bruise. The rifle would only be dangerous to the eye or other delicate areas. But in recent years, air-rifle manufacturers have come out with higher-cost, more powerful models. Prospective gun owners may be unaware that some newer model rifles have a punch close to that of a .38 caliber handgun, the same size the police carry.

Air rifles can be serious weapons! They should be handled with caution by responsible adults or by youngsters who are supervised by responsible adults, and never pointed at another person.

Accidental shootings have taken the lives of many young people and
innocent bystanders.

Did You Know?

A study was done by the Center to Prevent Handgun Violence of 266 accidental handgun shootings of youngsters under the age of 16. The accidents caused 140 deaths and 126 injuries. All the shootings happened between 1986 and 1988. Here is some of what the study showed:

• Most accidents happened at home. Half of the accidents happened at the victim's home. Another 30 percent happened at friends' houses. Only about 12 percent happened outdoors, in cars, or at workplaces.

• Most children shot at home wounded themselves or were shot by brothers or sisters. At a friend's house, the friend usually did the shooting.

• In almost half the shootings, the guns had been kept in bedrooms.

• In almost all the shootings, the guns belonged to the parents.

• It was found that in 8 out of 10 instances the injured people *and* the shooters were boys. Girls are seldom involved in handgun accidents.

• Children under the age of 4 usually shot themselves; 5- to 8-year-olds were most often shot by sisters or brothers; most 13- to 16-year-olds were shot by friends. Among 9- to 12-year-olds, the shooters were about equally split among friends, sisters or brothers, or the victims themselves.

• In 6 of every 10 cases, there was no adult in the house at the time the shooting happened.

Suicides

Young people who want to kill themselves don't need weapons to do it. According to studies in Washington and Tennessee, suicides are five times more likely to occur in homes with guns than in ones without. The likelihood of suicide goes up if the guns are left unlocked or loaded.

Doctors know that many times the urge to take one's life is impulsive. It may be a sudden reaction to something that has happened. When these strong feelings of suicide come up, if there's no easy way to do it, then there's a chance that the urge might pass. If a person does try suicide by some other means, such as taking too many pills, doctors might have a better chance of saving a person's life. The quick and massive wound made by a bullet is usually fatal.

"People who own firearms," say the scientists who did the study, "should think carefully about their reasons for keeping guns at home, against the chance it might someday be used in a suicide."

Fights and Family Violence

All families argue. The question is, *how* are conflicts resolved? What happens when people are angry at one another? Do people "act first" and think later?

Easy access to weapons has changed the way we look at conflict and family violence. In Colorado, a 14-year-old shot a 17-year-old neighbor to death in an argument over a baseball cap! It seems unbelievable, but things like this are happening—more and more.

Weapons in the home have also added more problems to already troubled families. This is especially true in cases of abuse where a family member may need protection from another family member. But using a weapon is always serious. Getting help, moving out, or calling the police would be the best ways to remain safe.

Some Final Thoughts

There are valid reasons to have weapons at home. It is also true that a large number of weapons in homes seldom cause problems. There are ways homeowners can reduce the risks associated with weapons.

Still, the *possibility* of accidents and family violence (even suicides) are more real when weapons are available. It is important to know the facts about gun safety, and to understand the responsibilities involved. It may help to decide if owning a weapon is right for your family.

Gang fights with fists and sticks are less likely to end with deaths.

Chapter 5

Danger in the Classroom

Each morning, about 100,000 young people get ready for high school. They pack their books and pocket their lunch money. But then they do something else. They strap on their gun! Over the last few years, more and more high schools have become shooting galleries—kids shooting dope and shooting guns at each other.

Gangs: A Serious Threat

Drugs and weapons are not new to schools. Neither are teenage gangs. If you've ever seen the 1950's movie "Blackboard Jungle" or the musical "West Side Story," you know that.

But back then, gangs fought mostly with their fists or with crude weapons. They sometimes carried single-shot weapons called *zipguns,* made from hardware store parts. Today's gangs are much more violent and more organized. Gang members carry police scanners to keep track of where the law is, and telephone beepers to set up drug deals. Their guns are high-tech and costly. They include Mac-10's, Uzis, and other army-type attack weapons that can seriously wound or kill more than one person in a short period of time.

One out of every four big-city school boards has decided to use metal detectors, like those at airports, at the main entrances to their buildings. Guns, knives, and other weapons are taken off the kids as they come through the school entryway.

Many of these schools also have a new kind of fire drill. Teachers and students practice hitting the floor at the sound of gunfire.

Not Just the Cities—Not Just the High Schools

The problem of weapons in schools is not only in the big cities. According to the U.S. government, *one high school student in every five—from big cities or small— carries a weapon of some kind.* One in 20 has a gun. That averages out to one gun in every class-sized group!

And for every gun, it's believed there are five to seven knives, Oriental fighting sticks, brass knuckles, chains, and other weapons.

Gangs in school make up a large part of the problem with weapons.

But gangs aren't the whole problem. There are many troubled youngsters who do not belong to any gang.

Like the boy in the first chapter, youngsters have taken hostages in more than 35 states. They've held more than 240 people at gunpoint. And even more disturbing is that in school today, when kids argue, many of them reach for weapons to solve their problems.

Problems with weapons are not limited to high schools. About a quarter (one in four) of incidents with guns occur in junior high schools, and more than 1 in 10 happen in elementary schools. There have even been weapons found in preschools. Guns have been taken away from children as young as five years old!

In one four-year survey of newspaper stories, it was found that 71 students and school workers died by gunfire, and another 201 were wounded. What's the cause of all the violence? Some experts blame it on the availability of weapons.

Easy-to-Get Weapons

No one under the age of 18 can legally own a gun. But with more than 200 million firearms in private hands, guns are amazingly easy to get.

ABC News wanted to see for themselves how available guns were in school. They put some young-looking undercover reporters in a typical school. Even though these "students" were new to the school, they were able to buy handguns from other students *within one day.* In fact, they had a choice of weapons, at different prices. "The youngster who had the guns had to be driven to us to make the deal," one reporter noted, "He wasn't old enough to drive a car himself!"

In another area, a reporter for *Newsweek* magazine asked local teens how easy it was to find guns in the neighborhood. "Easier to find than a copy of *Newsweek*," a teen told him.

Where do all these weapons come from? Some are stolen, but studies show that a large percentage of the guns in school belong to parents or other adults in the family. They are simply brought from home.

Why do so many of today's teens feel they need to carry weapons? Experts in teen behavior give these answers:

A Pocketful of Power

All young people like to be admired for being in control. They also like to have others take them seriously. Unfortunately, many youngsters don't believe in their own abilities. They try to get admiration and respect by carrying weapons. One young man put it this way, "When I had a gun or a knife, nobody could touch me."

Sadly, the young man made this statement at a state prison, where he's serving a life term for shooting a school official.

Teens in gangs feel a sense of power when they carry guns.

All the Kids Do It!

Teenagers are naturals at playing "follow the leader." They are often strongly influenced by peer pressure. But most of the fads they copy from their friends, like wearing baseball caps backward or jeans with torn knees, are harmless. Carrying weapons, on the other hand, is dangerous. Still, there are kids who carry weapons just because their friends do. They want to be accepted, so they take their chances.

Gang members often have to carry weapons as a condition of membership. It's part of the gang rules. It's also a way gang leaders keep their members from going to the police. "Before you tell the police about our illegal weapons," say the leaders, "remember that you carry, too."

Sometimes little children pack a gun or a knife so they can be like a big sister or brother. They may not be aware of the danger. It's sad to think that they look up to the very siblings who can get them killed.

The Answer to Life's Problems

Some experts who study juvenile behavior say that society has taught young people that violence is the way to solve problems. And every time the star in an action movie "blows away" the bad guys and walks off a hero, or the bad guys are cheered by their friends and escape police action, that lesson is reinforced.

Self-defense

Perhaps the most tragic reason of all that some young people carry weapons is self-defense. Isn't it time for society to take action when a young person feels the need to defend himself or herself against the weapon carried by another kid? Protection was the reason one 15-year-old gave for having a powerful .357 Magnum pistol in his bookbag. He never imagined that the gun would go off as he reached inside. But a shot did fire. It went right through the chest of one student nearby, and killed a second person.

Today's schools are facing weapons problems like never before. But there is hope. Many parents and concerned citizens are working hard to come up with some solutions. You'll read about some of their ideas in the next chapter.

James Brady and his wife Sarah applaud the passing of the Brady Bill, which promotes stronger gun restrictions.

Chapter 6

Calling for an End to Weapons Violence

Most parents and adults love children. They hate—and will find ways to fight—anything that seriously threatens the young.

Weapons violence at home and in school is exactly that kind of threat. Here are some steps parents, teachers, police, and other adults—with the help of young people—have begun to take.

Get Tough!

As you walk into certain Chicago schools, you'll find yourself walking into Operation SAFE (Schools Are For Education). It's a fast-moving, hit-and-run, anti-weapons program put together by the Chicago school system.

The heart of the program is a set of *portable* metal detectors. Chicago School Safety Director George Sams tells why portables are used: "A lot of schools want to put detectors in every school and use them every day," says Sams. "It won't work. If kids know they have to pass through a detector and that the detector will always be in the same place, they'll get the guns in through windows or back doors."

Instead, Sams' detectors are always on the move, popping up where least expected. So far, the program seems to be working.

Another key part of the SAFE program is a linkup between city police and school building guards. Under the law, police officers can't search a person unless they have a good reason to believe he or she is a lawbreaker.

School guards work under a looser set of rules. They can search a student just because they have a hunch he or she might be up to something. But they lack a police officer's power to make an arrest.

Under the linkup, the guards use their search power to stop and search young people as police stand by and watch. If a weapon is found, the police officer is right there to make an arrest.

In other "get tough" programs, *parents* are arrested if a child gets hold of a gun they own and is hurt or uses the weapon in a crime. The parents can go to jail, even though they took no active part in a crime!

Classes in gun safety are being attended by more women and young people than ever before.

Gun owners' groups think laws that hold parents responsible for their children's involvement with guns are unfair. "A child is five times as likely to drown as to be hurt with a firearm," they argue. "Yet no one is making laws against pool owners." But regardless of the protest, the laws have gone into effect. Many people feel very strongly about weapons safety—for the curious child as well as others who may be nearby.

Perhaps the toughest move of all is that more courts are trying teenagers as adults if they use weapons in a crime. That way, teens can be sent to the regular prisons instead of juvenile centers if found guilty. "Trying kids as adults is one of the few tools we have in the face of all this teen violence," says Robert Grant, a Colorado court official. "There are so many forces telling kids they can pick up a gun and it doesn't matter," he says. "We have to tell them it *does* matter."

Get Smart!

Gun owners' groups have their own programs, which often focus on weapons safety. The largest such group is the National Rifle Association (NRA).

The NRA puts on a program for elementary school children called "Eddie Eagle." The program uses coloring books to teach children to stay clear of any firearm they come across. More than 1.5 million youngsters, in some 3,000 schools, have had this program made available to them.

Another program, called STAR (Straight Talk About Risks) is put on by a group called The Center to Prevent Handgun Violence, a group favoring gun control. STAR has created activities and materials at four grade levels.

The youngest group (kindergarten through second grade) gets comic books that tell about the battle between two imaginary groups, the Yooks and the Zooks. The battle is over which side of the bread should be buttered.

While this story may seem ridiculous, its real aim is to teach young kids how to handle the angry feelings that lead to violence. The program also talks about weapons used in violent acts, and understanding the difference between real and make-believe violence.

Older STAR students (high school age) put on plays, and do study projects involving weapons and violence. The activities are more adult, but the learning goals are the same.

Get Involved!

In some communities, concerned parents have taken an active part in dealing with weapons violence in schools. They have formed Safety Watch programs in which parent squads patrol school hallways. Local businesses take part, too. They donate money, or allow parents to take time off from work with pay in order to participate in school patrols.

Neighborhood groups rally to stop the violence in schools and on the streets.

There's even a special educational group set up to research and deal with school violence and weapons problems. The National School Safety Council (NSSC) carries out studies, puts out newsletters and magazines, and offers teachers and other school officials training in how to keep peace in classrooms and in hallways. It may be helpful for teachers to be able to spot trouble before violence breaks out, and to have support services in place when needed. "Too many teachers come unprepared to deal with it all," says NSSC Director Ron Stephens. "Like the teacher who told me, 'I got my training the day the kid pointed a gun at my face.'"

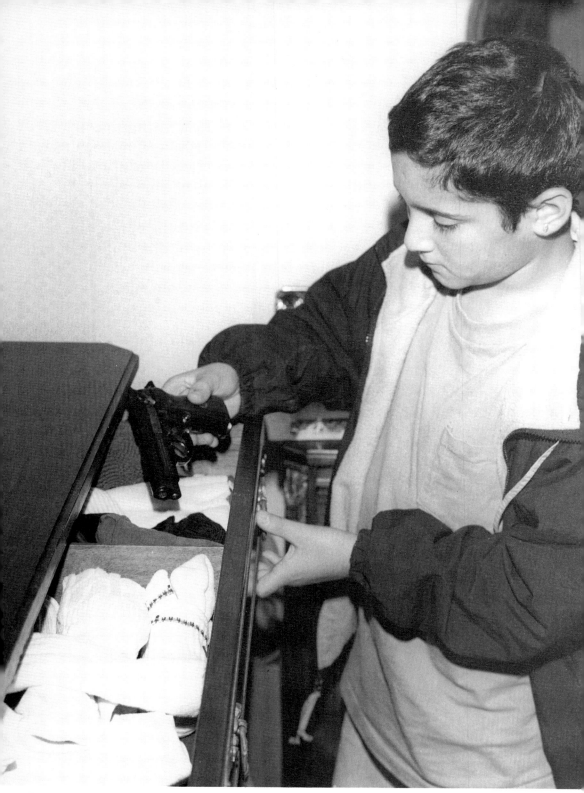

Weapons should never be kept within easy reach of young children.

Chapter 7

What YOU Can Do!

Adults are working hard to put an end to the problem of weapons in school and at home. But all the parents, police, school officials, lawmakers, and other adults put together don't have as much power as teens themselves to solve this problem. Here are some of the things YOU can do:

At Home

1. Stay away from guns and other weapons!
2. Keep sisters and brothers—especially younger ones—away from all weapons.
3. Talk with your parents about whether weapons are really needed at home. Remind them that there are risks, especially if:

- there are small children in the house
- there is anyone very excitable or who has talked of suicide
- your parents are untrained in the handling of weapons.

4. If the decision *is* to keep weapons in the house, ask your parents to follow these safety rules:

- Store the weapons in a locked case, cabinet, or closet. The harder the storage area is to break into, the better. A locked closet or wooden cabinet is better than a locked glass display case for keeping weapons from getting into the wrong hands.
- Store weapons *unloaded* and *uncocked* —be sure to check if there's a round left inside the gun. It's often the case that one bullet is in the firing chamber even when the bullet holding unit (magazine) has been taken out.
- Store bullets in a separate, locked case or container *away from the weapon.*
- Put a padlock, trigger lock, or other safety device on the weapon itself. These are sold in gun shops or sporting goods stores. Don't depend only on the gun's "safety" lever.
- Never hide a gun or other weapon in a bedside drawer, or under a mattress or pillow. These locations are sure to be checked out if a prowler breaks in, and they are also much too easy for children to get at!

- Do not store a weapon along with valuables, such as cash or jewelry. Burglars often get their guns this way.
- Learn proper gun care and cleaning. When an adult cleans a gun, he or she should be alone, in a safe place. Before cleaning, check the weapon *twice* to be sure it's unloaded.
- Have anyone old enough to handle a weapon attend a firearms safety class. These are offered by gun clubs, camps, and some school systems and police groups.
- Treat other weapons, such as knives, and bows and arrows, with similar care and caution.

5. If you know that someone is mishandling a weapon, get away, and tell an adult as soon as possible. If there is an accident involving a weapon, dial 911 and tell the operator that you have a police or medical emergency.

In School

1. Remember that there is *no* good reason to have a weapon with you in school. Never bring one to school!

2. Tell your friends you are against weapons in school.

3. If you see or know someone has a weapon, don't let him or her think you are impressed. Tell a teacher or other adult, either openly or by placing a note in the person's mailbox. (You don't have to give your name.) Even though the youngster may

Find someone to talk to if you feel threatened in school. You may not
be able to handle a dangerous situation alone.

get in trouble, you may be doing him or her, as well as others, a big favor.

4. If you are threatened with a weapon, do *not* try to fight back. Give the person whatever he or she wants, and report it to the authorities right afterward.

For Yourself

If *YOU* feel the need to pack a weapon, listen to the message from a young man named Chris Hans. Hans was interviewed on an ABC-TV news show.

Hans, a 14-year-old straight-A student in a good school, began to carry weapons when he started having problems with his parents and teachers. He didn't feel he could tell anyone about these problems. But with a gun or a knife in his possession, Chris felt powerful, in charge. He thought he could overcome any difficulty.

One day, Chris was especially upset and confused. He didn't think about asking for help. He didn't know anyone would be willing to listen to what he had to say. He decided to use the power he carried in his pocket. He walked into his school with a loaded gun and knocked on a teacher's door. When the unsuspecting teacher opened it, Chris shot her to death. Then he went down the hall and shot the vice principal. Fortunately, the vice principal lived, but he needed several serious operations. Chris was arrested, tried, convicted, and sent to jail.

Since the shootings, Chris Hans has had a lot of time to think about what he did— and he'll have a lot more. His sentence is 230 years behind bars!

The reporter asked Chris what advice he had for other youngsters, who might also be tempted to use weapons to solve their problems.

"Tell someone how you feel," said Chris, "and if that person won't listen, tell someone else, and then someone else. Find someone who will listen. Because if you don't, things will get a lot worse, real quick."

Glossary—*Explaining New Words*

action toys Group of toys that includes guns and other weapons, usually marketed to young boys.

assault Physical attack on someone.

debate Discussion of a question or issue. Arguments for and against are given in turn.

firearm Rifle, shotgun, or handgun.

gun control The idea that private ownership of guns should be more regulated by law. Under most proposed plans, the private ownership of handguns would be banned and rifle ownership would be more tightly controlled.

handgun Pistol or revolver.

martial arts Methods of fighting that use the hands and feet as weapons, developed by the Chinese, Japanese, Koreans, and other Far Eastern peoples. Karate is one form.

metal detector Machine that uses magnets to sound an alarm when there is a metal object present. Detectors are made in both walk-through and hand-held units.

Oriental stars Sharply pointed, star-shaped blades.

Oriental sticks Martial arts weapon made up of two sticks connected by a short chain.

pros and cons Arguments for and against an issue.

Right to Bear Arms Section of the United States Constitution that ensures a citizen's right to have guns to defend freedom.

suicide Taking of one's own life.

switchblade Specially made pocketknife that can be opened very quickly, using only one hand.

weapon Gun, knife, or any other item used to cause harm or damage.

Where to Get Information

Eddie Eagle Program
National Rifle Association (NRA)*
1600 Rhode Island Avenue, NW
Washington, DC 20036

STAR Program
Center to Prevent Handgun Violence*
1225 Eye Street NW
Washington, DC 20005

National School Safety Center
4165 Thousand Oaks Boulevard, Suite 290
Westlake Village, CA 91362

U.S. Department of Justice
Washington, DC 20530

Local law enforcement offices can often provide
further information on weapons issues in your area.

* Note: These organizations are heavily involved in
the debate over gun control. Materials they publish
may present information in a way that favors their
position. Read with care!

For Further Reading

Church, George J. "The Other Arms Race." *Time,* February 6, 1989, pp. 21–26.

Imbimbo, T. "Playing it Cool" (Violence Prevention for Adolescents). *Seventeen,* February, 1990, p. 40.

Katz, L.G. "How TV Violence Affects Kids." *Parents,* January 1991, p. 113.

Lacayo, Richard. "Under Fire." *Time,* January 29, 1990, pp. 16–23.

Landau, Elaine. *Teenage Violence.* Englewood Cliffs, NJ: Julian Messner, 1990.

Licata, Renora. *Everything You Need to Know about Anger.* New York: Rosen Publishing Group, 1992.

Treanor, William W., and Bijlefeld, Marjolign. *Kids & Guns: A Child Safety Scandal.* Washington, DC: The American Youth Work Center and The Educational Fund to End Handgun Violence, 1989.

Woods, Geraldine. *The Right to Bear Arms.* New York: Franklin Watts, 1986.

"Young and Deadly—The Rise in Teen Violence." *Scholastic Update,* April 5, 1991. Entire issue devoted to this topic.

Index

About the Author

A native of New York City and graduate of City College of New York, Jay Schleifer taught for five years in the New York school system with an emphasis on Special Education. He was editor of *Know Your World*, a high/low publication, for five years, and has authored more than 20 high/low books on a variety of topics. Jay now works as a publishing company executive and lives in the Midwest.

Photo Credits

Cover photo by Dick Smolinski.
Photo on page 2: AP/Wide World; pages 9, 36, 41: © Douglas Burrows/Gamma Liaison; page 12: © Mike Okoniewski; pages 17, 25, 50: © Jon Levy/Gamma Liaison; pages 20, 29, 47: © Paul Howell/Gamma Liaison; page 44: © Terry Ashe/Gamma Liaison; page 52: Stuart Rabinowitz; page 56: Mary Lauzon.

Design/Production: Blackbirch Graphics, Inc.